The Great Meeting is On!

KORAN QUESTIONS FOR MOORISH AMERICANS

NOBLE DREW ALI

Founder of

MOORISH SCIENCE TEMPLE OF AMERICA

Transcribed and edited by Dennis Logan

[2021]

Moorish American Prayer

ALLAH the Father of the Universe, the Father of Love, Truth, Peace, Freedom and Justice.

ALLAH is my Protector, my Guide, and my Salvation by night and by day, through His Holy Prophet, DREW ALI. (Amen).

Koran Questions for Moorish Children

1. Who made you? ALLAH
2. Who is ALLAH? ALLAH is the Father of the Universe.
3. Can we see Him?   No.
4. Where is the nearest place we can meet Him?   In the heart.
5. Who is Noble Drew Ali?   He is ALLAH's Prophet.
6. What is a Prophet?   A Prophet is a Thought of Allah manifested in the flesh.
7. What is the duty of a Prophet?   To save nations from the wrath of ALLAH.
8. Who is the founder of the MOORISH SCIENCE TEMPLE OF AMERICA?   Noble Drew Ali.
9. What year was the MOORISH SCIENCE TEMPLE OF AMERICA founded? 1913 A.D.
10.   Where?   Newark, New Jersey.
11.   Where was NOBLE DREW ALI born?   In the State of North Carolina, 1886.
12.   What is his nationality? Moorish-American.

13. What is your nationality? Moorish-American.

14. Why are we Moorish-Americans? Because we are descendants of Moroccans and born in America.

15. For what purpose was the Moorish Science Temple of America Founded? For the uplifting of fallen humanity.

16. How did the Prophet begin to uplift the Moorish Americans? By teaching them to be themselves.

17. What is our religion? Islamism.

18. Is that a new, or is that the old time religion? Old time religion.

19. What kind of a flag is the Moorish? It is a red flag with a five pointed green star in the center.

20. What do the five points represent? Love, Truth, Peace, Freedom and Justice.

21. How old is our flag? It is over 10,000 years old.

22. Which is our Holy Day? Friday.

23. Why? Because Friday is the day on which man was formed in flesh, and it was on Friday when He departed out of flesh.

24. Who was Jesus? He was a Prophet of Allah.
25. Where was He born? In Bethlehem, of Judah, in the House of David.
26. Who were His Father and Mother? Joseph and Mary.
27. Will you give in brief the line (genealogy) through which Jesus came? Some of the Great Fathers through which Jesus came are: Abraham, Boaz by Ruth, Jesse, King David, Solomon, Hezekiah and Joseph by Mary.
28. Why did ALLAH send Jesus to this earth? To save the Israelites from the iron-hand oppression of the pale-skin nations of Europe, who were governing a portion of Palestine at that time.
29. How long has that been? About two thousand years ago.
30. What was the nationality of Ruth? Ruth was a Moabitess.
31. What is the modern name for Moabites? Moroccans.
32. Where is the Moroccan Empire? Northwest Amexem.
33. What is the modern name for Amexem? Africa.

34. What is the title given to our ruler in Morocco?   Sultan.

35. Where do we get the name Jesus?   From the East.

36. What does the name Jesus mean?   Jesus means Justice.

37. Did the Angel give to the Child that was called Jesus a Holy name?   Yes but it cannot be used by those who are slaves to sin.

38. What is an Angel?   An Angel is a thought of Allah manifested in human flesh.

39. What are Angels used for? To carry messages to the four corners of the world, to all nations.

40. What is our Prophet to us? He is an Angel of ALLAH who was sent to bring us the Everlasting Gospel of ALLAH.

41. What is the Everlasting Gospel?   It is a Saving Power that comes from ALLAH through our Ancient Fathers, by His Prophet.

42. What is the Covenant of the Great GOD-ALLAH?   Honor thy Father and thy Mother, that thy days may be long upon the Earthland which the Lord thy GOD-ALLAH hath given thee.

43.   At what age did Jesus begin to teach?   At the age of twelve.

44.   Where did He teach? India, Africa and Europe.

45.   How long did He teach? Eighteen years.

46.   What did Jesus say that would make you free? TRUTH.

47.   What is TRUTH?   TRUTH is Aught.

48.   What is Aught? Aught is ALLAH.

49.   Can TRUTH change? TRUTH cannot change, or pass away.

50.   What other name do we give to TRUTH?   HOLY BREATH.

51.   What have you to say about HOLY BREATH?   All we can say it is Great. It is good. It was, it is, and evermore to be. AMEN.

52.   At what place on earth was the physical part of MAN formed?   In the Garden of Eden.

53.   Where is the Garden of Eden?   In the land of Canaan, in the City of Mecca.

54.   What is the modern name for the Garden of Eden? MECCAA.

55.   What is the name of the first Physical man? His name cannot be

used, only by Executive Rulers of the A.C. of the M.S.T. of A.

56.   What are the words of A.C. of the M. S. T. of A?   Adept Chamber of the Morrish Science Temple of America (3rd Heaven).

57.   Who were Adam and Eve? They are the mothers and fathers of the human family. Asiatics and Moslems.

58.   Where did they go?   They went into Asia.

59.   What is the modern name given to their children?   Asiatics.

60.   Who is guarding the Holy City of MECCA today to keep the unbelievers away?   Angels.

61.   What is the modern name for those Angels?   Asiatics.

62.   What is the shade of their skin?   Olive.

63.   Are the Moorish Americans any relation to those Angels?   Yes, we all have the same father and mother.

64.   Give five names that are given to the descendants of Adam and Eve: Lucifer, Satan, Devil, Dragon and Beast.

65.   What is the Devil some times called?   The Lower-self.

66. How many selves are there? Two.

67. Name them: Higher-self and Lower-self.

68. What people represent the Higher-self? The Angels who protect the Holy City of MECCA.

69. What people represent the Lower-self? Those who were cast out of the Holy City, and those who accept their teaching.

70. What is the Higher-self? The Higher-self is the Mother of virtues and the harmonies of life, and breeds Justice, Mercy, Love and Right.

71. Can the Higher-self pass away? No.

72. Why? Because it is ALLAH in Man.

73. What does the Lower-self breed? Hatred, Slander, Lewdness, Murders, Theft, and everything that harms.

74. What did the Higher-self say to the Lower-self at one time when He met Him? "Where are you going Satan?"

75. What was the answer that the Lower-self gave to the Higher-self? ("I am going to and fro the earth seeking whom I may devour.")

76. Has he finished his task of devouring? Yes.
77. When was His time declared out? When He nailed Jesus on the cross.
78. What are the last words Jesus uttered? It is finished.
79. What did He have reference to? He had reference to the end of Satan.
80. Did Jesus say that He would return to conquer Him? Yes.
81. What is the name of the person into whom Jesus was first reincarnated? Prophet MOHAMMED, the Conqueror.
82. Was Satan to be bound then? Satan was to be bound in part.
83. When was the head of Satan taken off? 1453 (Byzantine)
84. By whom? By Mohammed.
85. Name some of the marks that were put upon the MOORS of Northwest, by the European nations in 1774? Negro, Black, Colored and Ethiopia.
86. Negro, a name given to a river in West Africa by MOORS, because it contains black water.

87.   What is meant by the word Black?   Black according to science means death.

88.   What does the word colored mean?   Colored means anything that has been painted, stained, varnished or dyed.

89.   What does Ethiopia mean?   Ethiopia means something divided.

90.   Can a man be a Negro, Black, Colored or Ethiopian?   No.

91.   Why?   Because man is made in the Image and after the likeness of God, Allah.

92.   What title does Satan give Himself?   God.

93.   Will you define the word White?   White means Purity, Purity means God, and God means the Ruler of the Land.

94.   To whom do we refer to at times, as being the GREAT GOD?   ALLAH.

95.   Is the Devil made in the Image and Likeness of ALLAH?   No, he is the shadow of our lower-selves and will pass away.

96.   Who made the Devil?   Elohim.

97.   Who is Elohim? Elohim, is the Seven Creative Spirits that created everything that ever was, is, and evermore to be.

98.   What is Elohim sometimes called?   The SEVEN EYES of ALLAH.

99.   How many days are in the Circle?   Seven days.

100.   How many days are in a a creation? Seven days.

101.   According to Science, how many days are in a year?
       Seven days.

Questionnaire and Additional Laws for
The Moorish Americans
(BY THE PROPHET NOBLE DREW ALI)

ACT 1.-Grand Sheiks, and Governors and heads of all Temples, all Businesses; Each said Temple must be approved by the Prophet Noble Drew Ali. Before acting upon by any members, let it be finance property or any life of life that will cause the members to sacrifice finance, etc., that will cause the support of any group of members. Any former officer that violates these laws is subject to be removed from his office under heavy restriction, etc., by the Prophet or the Grand Sheik.

ACT 2.-All members are to attend their adept meetings and their public meetings promptly. If a member is found standing around on their meeting period, shall be fined $.50 on the first case, and on the second, he will be fined one dollar ($1.00), which will go on your emergency fund. If member is working his monthly dues must be paid, and if he has money in the bank he must subscribe for as much as he his able, to the Moorish Uplifting Fund, because it takes finance to uplift a Nation.

ACT 3.-It is lawful and devine duty of every good member if he is able in finance to aid me in saving the nation and if he does not, he is an enemy to the cause of uplifting his own people and Justice must catch you. Let it be he or she according to Love, Truth, Peace, Freedom and Justice as I have the power invested in my hands and I will have to enforce the law in order to save the nation.

ACT 4.-All members while making a public speech must not use any assertion against the American flag or speak radical against the church or any member of any organized group, because we are to teach Love, Truth, Peace, Freedom and Justice.

ACT 5.-All members must promptly attend their meetings and send their children to Sunday School, and the teacher must confirm himself to the questionary. And let every member exercise his five senses who is able to do so, because out from your Sunday School comes the guiders of the Nation.

ACT 6.-With us all members must proclaim their nationality and we are teaching our people their nationality and their Divine Creed that they may know that they are a part and partial of this said government, and know that they are not Negroes, Colored Folks, Black People or Ethiopians, because these names were given to slaves by slave holders in 1779 and lasted until 1865 during the time of slavery, but this is a new era of time now, and all men now must proclaim their free national name to be recognized by the government in which they live and the nations of the earth, this is the reason why Allah the Great God of the universe ordained Noble Drew Ali, the Prophet to redeem his people from their sinful ways. The Moorish Americans are the descendants of the ancient Moabites who inhabited the North Western and South Western shores of Africa.

ACT 7.-All members must promptly attend their meetings and become a part and a partial of all uplifting acts of the Moorish Science Temple. Members must pay their dues and keep in line with all necessities of the Moorish Science Temple, then you are entitled to the name of "Faithful." Husband, you must support your wife and children. Wife, you must obey your husband and take care of your children and look after the duties of your household. Sons and daughters must obey father and mother and be industrious and become part of the uplifting of fallen humanity. All Moorish Americans must keep their hearts and minds pure with love, and their bodies clean with water. This Divine Covenant is from your Holy Prophet Noble Drew Ali, through the guidance of his Father, God Allah.

The Great Meeting Is On!

ISLAM

ASIA

KORAN QUESTIONS FOR MOORISH AMERICANS

HUMANITY

PROPHET DREW ALI

THE CARES OF THE WORLD

SALVATION

NOBLE DREW ALI Founder of
MOORISH SCIENCE TEMPLE OF AMERICA
48 INCHES MT. CLEMENS, MI.
Price 50¢

Moorish American Prayer

ALLAH the Father of the Universe, the Father of Love, Truth, Peace, Freedom and Justice. ALLAH is my Protector, my Guide, and my Salvation by night and by day, through His Holy Prophet, DREW ALI. (Amen).

🌀 🌀 🌀

Koran Questions for Moorish Children

1. Who made you?   ALLAH.

2. Who is ALLAH?   ALLAH is the Father of the Universe.

3. Can we see Him?   No.

4. Where is the nearest place we can meet Him?   In the heart.

5. Who is Noble Drew Ali?   He is ALLAH'S Prophet.

6. What is a Prophet?   A Prophet is a Thought of Allah manifested in the flesh.

7. What is the duty of a Prophet?   To save nations from the wrath of ALLAH.

8. Who is the founder of the MOORISH SCIENCE TEMPLE OF AMFRICA?   Noble Drew Ali.

9. What year was the MOORISH SCIENCE TEMPLE OF AMERICA founded?   1913 A. D.

10. Where?   Newark, New Jersey.

11. Where was NOBLE DREW ALI born?   In the State of North Carolina, 1886.

12. What is his nationality?   Moorish-American.

13. What is your nationality?   Moorish-American.

14. Why are we Moorish-Americans?   Because we are descendants of Morrocans and born in America.

15. For what purpose was the Moorish Science Temple of America Founded?   For the uplifting of fallen humanity.

1

16. How did the Prophet begin to uplift the Moorish Americans? By teaching them to be themselves.

17. What is our religion? Islamism.

18. Is that a new, or is that the old time religion? Old time religion.

19. What kind of a flag is the Moorish? It is a red flag with a five pointed green star in the center.

20. What do the five points represent? Love, Truth, Peace, Freedom and Justice.

21. How old is our flag? It is over 10,000 years old.

22. Which is our Holy Day? Friday.

23. Why? Because Friday is the day on which man was formed in flesh, and it was on Friday when He departed out of flesh.

24. Who was Jesus? He was a Prophet of Allah.

25. Where was He born? In Bethlehem, of Judah, in the House of David.

26. Who were His Father and Mother? Joseph and Mary.

27. Will you give in brief the line (geneology) through which Jesus came? Some of the Great Fathers through which Jesus came are: Abraham, Boaz by Ruth, Jesse, King David, Solomon, Hezekiah and Joseph by Mary.

28. Why did ALLAH send Jesus to this earth? To save the Israelites from the iron-hand oppression of the pale-skin nations of Europe, who were governing a portion of Palestine at that time.

29. How long has that been? About two thousand years ago.

30. What was the nationality of Ruth? Ruth was a Moabitess.

31. What is the modern name for Moabites? Moroccans.

32. Where is the Morroccan Empire? Northwest Amexem.

33. What is the modern name for Amexem? Africa.

34. What is the title given to our ruler in Morocco? Sultan.

35. Where do we get the name Jesus? From the East.

2

36. What does the name Jesus mean? (Jesus means Justice.)

37. Did the Angel give to the Child that was called Jesus a Holy name? Yes, but it cannot be used by those who are slaves to sin.

38. What is an Angel? An Angel is a thought of ALLAH manifested in human flesh.

39. What are Angels used for? To carry messages to the four corners of the world, to all nations.

40. What is our Prophet to us? He is an Angel of ALLAH who was sent to bring us the Everlasting Gospel of ALLAH.

41. What is the Everlasting Gospel? It is a Saving Power that comes from ALLAH through our Ancient Fathers, by His Prophet.

42. What is the Covenant of the Great GOD-ALLAH? Honor thy Father and thy Mother, that thy days may be long upon the Earthland which the Lord thy GOD-ALLAH hath given thee.

43. At what age did Jesus begin to teach? At the age of twelve.

44. Where did He teach? India, Africa and Europe.

45. How long did He teach? Eighteen years.

46. What did Jesus say that would make you free? TRUTH.

47. What is TRUTH? TRUTH is Aught.

48. What is Aught? Aught is ALLAH.

49. Can TRUTH change? TRUTH cannot change, or pass away.

50. What other name do we give to TRUTH? HOLY BREATH.

51. What have you to say about HOLY BREATH? All we can say it is Great. It is good. It was, it is, and evermore to be. AMEN.

52. At what place on earth was the physical part of MAN formed? In the Garden of Eden.

53. Where is the Garden of Eden? (In the land of Canaan, in the City of Mecca.)

54. What is the modern name for the Garden of Eden? MECCA.

3

55. What is the name of the first Physical Man? (His name cannot be used, only by Executive Rulers of the A. C. of the M. S. T. of A.)

56. What are the words of A. C. of the M. S. T. of A? Adept Chamber of the Moorish Science Temple of America (3rd Heaven).

57. Who were Adam and Eve? They are the mothers and fathers of the human family. Asiatics and Moslems.

58. Where did they go? They went into Asia.

59. What is the modern name given to their children? Asiatics.

60. Who is guarding the Holy City of MECCA today to keep the unbelievers away? Angels.

61. What is the modern name for those Angels? Asiatics.

62. What is the shade of their skin? Olive.

63. Are the Moorish Americans any relation to those Angels? Yes, we all have the same father and mother.

64. Give five names that are given to the descendants of Adam and Eve: Lucifer, Satan, Devil, Dragon and Beast.

65. What is the Devil some times called? The Lower-self.

66. How many selves are there? Two.

67. Name them: Higher-self and Lower-self.

68. What people represent the Higher-self? The Angels who protect the Holy City of MECCA.

69. What people represent the Lower-self? Those who were cast out of the Holy City, and those who accept their teaching.

70. What is the Higher-self? The Higher-self is the Mother of virtues and the harmonies of life, and breeds Justice, Mercy, Love and Right.

71. Can the Higher-self pass away? No.

72. Why? Because it is ALLAH in MAN.

73. What does the Lower-self breed? Hatred, Slander, Lewdness, Murders, Theft, and everything that harms.

74. What did the Higher-self say to the Lower-self at one time when He met Him? "Where are you going Satan?"

4

75. What was the answer that the Lower-self gave to the Higher-self? "I am going to and fro the earth seeking whom I may devour."

76. Has he finished his task of devouring? Yes.

77. When was His time declared out? When He nailed Jesus on the cross.

78. What are the last words Jesus uttered? It is finished.

79. What did He have reference to? He had reference to the end of Satan.

80. Did Jesus say that He would return to conquer Him? Yes.

81. What is the name of the person into whom Jesus was first reincarnated? Prophet MOHAMMED, the Conqueror.

82. Was Satan to be bound then? Satan was to be bound in part.

83. When was the head of Satan taken off? 1453 (Byzantine).

84. By whom? By Mohammed.

85. Name some of the marks that were put upon the MOORS of Northwest, by the European nations in 1774? Negro, Black, Colored and Ethiopia.

86. Negro, a name given to a river in West Africa by MOORS, because it contains black water.

87. What is meant by the word Black? Black according to science means death.

88. What does the word colored mean? Colored means anything that has been painted, stained, varnished or dyed.

89. What does Ethiopia mean? Ethiopia means something divided.

90. Can a man be a Negro, Black, Colored or Ethiopian? No.

91. Why? Because man is made in the Image and after the likeness of God, Allah.

92. What title does Satan give Himself? God.

93. Will you define the word White? White means Purity, Purity means God, and God means the Ruler of the Land.

5

94. To whom do we refer to at times, as being the GREAT GOD? ALLAH.

95. Is the Devil made in the Image and Likeness of ALLAH? No, he is the shadow of our lower-selves and will pass away.

96. Who made the Devil? Elohim.

97. Who is Elohim? Elohim, is the Seven Creative Spirits that created everything that ever was, is, and evermore to be.

98. What is Elohim sometimes called? The SEVEN EYES of ALLAH.

99. How many days are in the Circle? Seven days.

100. How many days are in a creation? Seven days.

101. According to Science, how many days are in a year? Seven days.

Questionnaire and Additional Laws for

The Moorish Americans

(BY THE PROPHET NOBLE DREW ALI)

ACT 1.—Grand Shieks, and Governors and heads of all Temples, all Businesses; Each said Temple must be approved by the Prophet Noble Drew Ali. Before acting upon by any members, let it be finance property or any line of life that will cause the members to sacrifice finance, etc., that will cause the support of any group of members. Any former officer that violates these laws is subject to be removed from his office under heavy restriction, etc., by the Prophet or the Grand Shiek.

ACT 2.—All members are to attend their adept meetings and their public meetings promptly. If a member is found standing around on their meeting period, shall be fined 50¢ on the first case, and on the second, he will be fined one dollar ($1.00), which will go on your emergency fund. If member is working his monthly dues must be paid, and if he has money in the bank he must subscribe for as much as he is able, to the Moorish Uplifting Fund, because it takes finance to uplift a Nation.

ACT 3.—It is lawful and devine duty of every good member if he is able in finance, to aid me in saving the nation and if he does not, he is an enemy to the cause of uplifting his own people and Justice must catch you. Let it be he or she according to Love, Truth, Peace, Freedom and Justice as I have the power invested in my hands and I will have to enforce the law in order to save the nation.

ACT 4.—All members while making a public speech must not use any assertion against the American flag or speak radical against the church or any member of any organized group, because we are to teach Love, Truth, Peace, Freedom and Justice.

ACT 5.—All members must promptly attend their meetings and send their children to Sunday School, and the teacher must confirm himself to the questionary. And let every member exercise his five senses who is able to do so, because out from your Sunday School comes the guiders of the Nation.

ACT 6.—With us all members must proclaim their nationality and we are teaching our people their nationality and their Divine Creed that they may know that they are a part and partial of this said government, and know that they are not Negroes, Colored Folks, Black People or Ethiopians, because these names were given to slaves by slave holders in 1779 and lasted until 1865 during the time of slavery, but this is a new era of time now, and all men now must proclaim their free national name to be recognized by the government in which they live and the nations of the earth, this is the reason why Allah the Great God of the universe ordained Noble Drew Ali, the Prophet to redeem his people from their sinful ways. The Moorish Americans are the descendants of the ancient Moabites who inhabited the North Western and South Western shores of Africa.

ACT 7.—All members must promptly attend their meetings and become a part and a partial of all uplifting acts of the Moorish Science Temple. Members must pay their dues and keep in line with all necessities of the Moorish Science Temple, then you are entitled to the name of "Faithful." Husband, you must support your wife and children. Wife, you must obey your husband and take care of your children and look after the duties of your household. Sons and daughters must obey father and mother and be industrious and become part of the uplifting of fallen humanity. All Moorish Americans must keep their hearts and minds pure with love, and their bodies clean with water. This Divine Covenant is from your Holy Prophet Noble Drew Ali, through the guidance of his Father, God Allah.

OUR AUTHORITY

(COPY)
Book 521   PAGE 579
            State of Illinois, Cook County ss
            No. 10105905

Filed For Record

CORPORATION — Religious — Affidavit of Organization
Form No. 1099.
STATE OF ILLINOIS,
County of COOK

ss

1928 AUG. 1 PM 252
AND RECORDED IN
BOOK   PAGE

I, NOBLE DREW ALI,...................................Recorder

Salomea Jasconowskie

MOORISH SCIENCE TEMPLE OF AMERICA...............held

at...............Chicago...............in the County of COOK...............

and State of Illinois, on the..................20th..................day of

...............July...............A. D. 1928, for that purpose, the fol-

lowing persons were appointed..................SHIEKS..................

..................................according to the rules and usages of such

MOORISH SCIENCE TEMPLE OF AMERICA

do solemnly swear that at the meeting of the members of the
NOBLE DREW ALI, MEALY EL, SMALL BEY LOVETT
BEY AND FOREMAN BEY. The Moorish Science Temple
of America deriving its power and authority from the Great
Koran of Mohammed to propogate the faith and extend the
learning and truth of the Great Prophet of ALI in America.
To appoint and consecrate missionaries of the prophet and
to establish the faith of Mohammed in America.

And said MOORISH SCIENCE TEMPLE OF AMERI-
CA adopted as its corporate name, the following MOORISH
SCIENCE TEMPLE OF AMERICA.................................

And at said meeting, this affiant acted as Presiding
officer Subscribed and Sworn to Before me.

..................20th.................................day of

...............July...........................A. D. 1928.......

Drew Ali.................................

Roberta W. Counull
                    Notary Public

See Hurd's Rev. Stat., Chap. 32, 36. *Our appointed *Or Wardens
        vestrymen, or whatever name they may adopt

Printed in the USA
CPSIA information can be obtained
at www.ICGtesting.com
LVHW050751300724
786794LV00032B/444

9 781952 900488